1 MONTH OF FREE READING

at

www.ForgottenBooks.com

By purchasing this book you are eligible for one month membership to ForgottenBooks.com, giving you unlimited access to our entire collection of over 1,000,000 titles via our web site and mobile apps.

To claim your free month visit:

www.forgottenbooks.com/free7852

ISBN 978-0-483-85631-8
PIBN 10007852

This book is a reproduction of an important historical work. Forgotten Books uses state-of-the-art technology to digitally reconstruct the work, preserving the original format whilst repairing imperfections present in the aged copy. In rare cases, an imperfection in the original, such as a blemish or missing page, may be replicated in our edition. We do, however, repair the vast majority of imperfections successfully; any imperfections that remain are intentionally left to preserve the state of such historical works.

SONNETS

BY

FANNY PURDY PALMER

PAUL ELDER & COMPANY
PUBLISHERS · SAN FRANCISCO

TO MY DAUGHTER
HENRIETTA

I INSCRIBE THESE RECORDS OF
SCENES IN WHICH WE HAVE BEEN TOGETHER,
AND OF THOUGHTS AND FANCIES
WHICH WE HAVE SO OFTEN
DISCUSSED IN LOVING
SYMPATHY

CONTENTS

SONNETS OF CALIFORNIA

Never Knew."

CALIFORNIA

I.

DISTINCTIVELY adorned, with joy caressed
By sun and wind, for Her exalted seat
The rocks are gold-inlaid, and at Her feet
An Ocean brings its argosies to rest.
Pensive Her mien, for close within her breast
Forest and stream and shifting sands secrete
The stories of adventurous lives replete
With daring hopes staked on some baffled Quest.
Thro' meadows green She muses on her past
When Mission bells ring out their call to prayer;
Or, rapt in Self, surveys Her heavens that brood
O'er lofty Peaks with lonely Valleys vast—
The bees drone heavy in the honeyed air,
The Mourning Dove laments in solitude.

CALIFORNIA

THE stolid Indian's tread had crossed this
    land,
    Crossed and recrossed and left but scanty
    trace,
When, from afar, men of a bolder race
Sighted its shores, set foot upon its sand
With praise to God; In haste, as rovers, planned
Return: An interval—and then—gold lace,
Doubloons, fandangoes, señoritas' grace!
But, steadily, by plain and pass, a band
Of Fortune's soldiers armored for the age
With wit and vigor; for the Wilds endowed
With prescient resource, strength of stubborn wills,
Came pressing on to this—their heritage,
Seeing in dreams its future cities proud
Of palaces made worthy of their hills.

6

CALIFORNIA

III.

COMPOSITE, unassimilable, crude
 As Her unsmelted ores, the social state
 Where differing races struggle to create
 Their planes of life anew. Needs must
  intrude
Fallacious dreams, false reasonings which delude
Th' unpracticed mind; But, She'll in time be great
Enough to find, amid the turns of fate,
The Way to shun—the Way to be pursued.
Purples and gold in groves and orchards glow,
And, housed in pearl, the Abalones cling
To the wet rocks: Mid fairest scenes at home
Her people dwell, and tides of travel flow
From ends of earth;—Such various folk they bring
As once they brought up to the Cæsars' Rome.

THE MEADOW-LARK

Sweet Master of Strange Dialects of Tune.

ALERT his eye, half hushed his liquid note
   When twilight gathers where the barley
     green
   For his rough nest provides a doubtful
     screen;
But bold and high bursts from his swelling throat—
In praise of the brown mate not far remote—
His morning lay,—a loud rejoicing pæan
Wherein the joy of living well has been
Resolved anew. Later, at times he'll quote
Some jargon, with a muffled trill to add
Confidingly, "I'm one of you, Not bad'
Ripe cherries, eh!" Then, settled for a stay,
He brings his friends, melodiously gay,
To revel with him while the world's in tune
And play the Bacchant 'mong the grapes at noon.

A SEA-GULL

E WAS not born a safe and happy bird
To pledge his mate in April evenings how
Sweet fruits would hang at length from
   yon slim bough
To feed their callow brood. Too soon he heard
From an imperilled nest the fateful word
That calls each to its own: 'Twas his to know
The driving gale, the spent ship's battered prow,
The wild tide-vigil; and so, undeterred
He gave the waves his wings! His frightened heart
Of all those thundering breakers felt the start!
No shelter but the cliff for his white breast
Where, panting, mid the cold salt spray 'tis pressed:
And last a wave-washed beach and wreck-strewn
   shore
And beaten bird—whose stormy life is o'er.

MY GARDEN BY THE SEA

I MADE a garden by th' unmindful Sea
So close, the breakers tossed among the
flowers
Their flecks of foam! Yet, in serener hours
Profuse and brilliant, wonderful to see,
My flowers outvied the waves' temerity:
Lamarques and Banksias flung their bloom in
showers;
From the Old World—with legends for their
dowers—
Iris and Cinerarias: Glad to be
The gayest of them all Geraniums red
As Cardinals' hats their dazzling clusters spread,
And Chinese Lilies stood in rows—so white
You saw them even in the darkest night.
All was most fair! and then—th' unmindful Sea
With its grey Breath effaced my flowers and me!

MONTEREY CYPRESS

SENTINELS old, posted along the way
 Beyond my garden's bounds — a rugged Band
  Of Natives staunch, born to the salt sea sand,
The fog's embrace, the Winter wind's rough play!
In sombre garb they greet their Captain grey
When south winds lash his tides to loud command!—
The tokens of his rage they understand
And shuddering at their posts his Will obey.
Nothing to them is man's intrusive care,
For lives apart they lead beside the sea
Rooted in creviced cliffs, where breakers dare
Stretch wind-curled arms to clasp the twisted tree
That, yielding, harkens to the roar and moan
Of the wild ocean when it calls its own!

WHEN THE OVERLAND STARTS EAST

GOOD-BYES all spoken: One last restless
    light
Still flashing on the gear till word shall tell
The moment come when, with slow
    clanging bell,
And like some living creature stretched for flight,
The long train moves beyond our straining sight.
The night wind's in our faces. "Is it well,"
It cries, "to part thus? Fear ye not Farewell?"
'Tis true we fear it. Few things can requite
Th' attachments we abandon. Speeds the train!—
Grappling with mountains, plunged in snow-sheds
    grim,
Skimming the desolate Lake, across the plain
Hastening to city brisk and village trim:
Ocean to Ocean traversed!—We again
Turn to the mountain Wall, the sunset's Rim.

LA JOLLA

A BARE, brown coast that curves to meet
     the Sea,
     With caves and cliffs where gulls and cur-
     lews dwell,
And riven rocks whose wave-worn tables tell
The Past's long story unforgetfully.
High tides that hold their daily Jubilee
With flying foam and roar, that leap and swell
Till the swift Ebb drowning its own wild knell
Bears all the billows back regretfully;
The sky is blue above, the sea below,—
If care or sorrow ever crossed thy lot
Rest here and drink of sea and sky thy fill,
Learn Ocean's Secrets when the tides are low,
And hear the lark sing! while in yonder spot
The Silent Sunrise crowns the lonely hill.

IN A CANYON

WHICH way leads out? Where was the
    entrance to
    This strange domain? No answer but the
    sound
Of your own footfall in the narrow bound
Whose lofty walls close round you to the blue:
Here, in the shade a Shape looks down on you;—
A Giant Warrior crouched against a mound,
His narrow brow with one tall Yucca crowned
He waits, till ancient foes their feuds renew.
There, in the sun up arid heights afar
Clambers the lonely desert's "bearded brood,"
While thick along your way the Shooting Star
With its pale grace and scent of solitude,—
A Spirit more than blossom — flowers alone
Within the Canyon's jealous heart, unknown.

THE CARMEL VALLEY FROM THE RIVER'S MOUTH

FIND me new feelings, Heart! New vision,
    Eyes!
    For words befitting beauty that I've
      brought
From other scenes, for this avail me naught.
Beyond these dunes, where wooded Mountains rise,
The sense beholds the Earth in Heaven's disguise
And, stirred, recalls — thro' vernal meadows fraught
With broideries of flowers in symbols wrought —
The mediæval dream of Paradise!
Mantled in Manzanita lies the way
Toward the Vale: the light of golden rose
That after sunset serves the day's delay
Is over all: the shadowy river flows —
Bearing, along the silvery sands it laves,
The Willows' message to the Ocean's waves.

ROSES

SAFRANOS for the young and fortunate
Who, with the roses, squander on an hour
The bloom that comes but once to heart
    or flower:
And fair Arguello's rose for those who wait
Like her for love's return importunate.
The lavish Banksias for the dreamer's bower,
And Brides significant their gifts to shower
On maids who lead processionals of fate.
With flaring petals wide the Cherokee
Takes to its heart the moonlight's mystery;
And there's a rose dear to fastidious eyes,
In whose complex repose perfection lies
Beauty's excuse for being to convey—
'T is called the Madam Abel Chatenay.

SEA FOG

IMMERGED are all the mountain tops in
    grey
    Of mists that cling to sloping pastures
    green,
And on the crests, the lifting rifts between,
The shrouded pines appear, to fade away
Like Phantoms clad in Penitent's array.
The sky is lost, the fortress'd point, and e'en
The sated sea. In sight of reefs unseen
A ghostly ship to windward shuns the Bay.
The moisture gathers in the muffled Wood
Where ferns refreshed their plumy branches spread,
And Lilacs bud, as if they understood
This medium of Dreams wherein we tread
Beset by sparkling chains the spiders spin,—
While from th' unsated sea the fog rolls in.

17

NEW YEAR'S EVE

THE darkening day that ends the dying Year
Broods upon dusky wings within my room,
And at the open door, where roses bloom,
Wan, wavering Forms, with faltering
    steps, appear
From far and travel worn, to find me Here!
They are the vanished Years, which reassume
The guise they wore, peopling the twilight gloom
With Memories more than heavy heart can bear:
Yet stay, poor Wanderers, till the New Year's born
While waning Moon sinks in the placid Sea,
And the first promise of a laggard morn
Brings to dejected mood its remedy.
But, ere the light, back—back to whence you sped!
For the Old Years, pale ghosts, are dead—are dead.

POST MERIDIEM

"A Sonnet is a coin; its face reveals
The soul."

COMPENSATION

OO passionate Heart, resenting in thy Day
Of lordly hopes and limitless despair
Life's lost illusions, let me lead you where
Sweet Nature hides her waste; in careless
    way
Her waste and losses hides: In time of May
'Round nests forsook in shivering orchards bare
She flings her wreaths abloom, and, blithe of air,
Our trust entreats for what the Orioles say!
Comes Autumn brown and lo! a cheat supreme
Where blossom's pledge was false to blighted fruit!
Yet, ah! the rosy transport of the Dream
Before the petals fell or song was mute,
The faith elate, th' apocalyptic Day,
Compensate for the life lived after May!

QUENCH NOT THE FIRES

QUENCH not the fires that burn within the
    soul
E'en though the world smiles chill upon
    their glow:
But feed those lonely fires which flicker low
With all that's best out of thy fortune's dole:
Thine ease consume, content, and proud control,
And love—dear love! Some hearts must bear to
  know
This last bereavement—love consumed—if so
They feed the fires which burn within the soul
Its utmost to inspire. The flames may blind,
To ashes turn the toys thou did'st adore;
But trust the light that shines. Fear not to mind
The inner impulse urging thee from shore
On stormy ventures. Quicken thy desires
For ports beyond thy sight. Quench not the fires!

TEMPERAMENT

STRONG souls, who seek through rending tumult name
For their emotions — eagle-beakèd brood —
Create 'twixt hope and fear some symbol rude
Of that conceived within. For love and fame —
Careless of shallow praise or shallower blame —
They shape the visioned forms which still elude
The comprehension of the multitude,
And serve, devout, the Offspring which they claim.
These are the souls who seek the Absolute
In high conceits: entreat their verity
Of human lives, of stars, and mountains mute;
Limners elect — high priests of ecstasy —
They mold, with reverent hand and ardent heart,
Truth's bold reflection fair, — the mask is Art.

CHOOSING

"When half-gods go, the gods arrive."

NOT to the cricket shrill through lonesome
eve
Nor to the crimson bough above the pool —
Mere incidents of Summer's passing rule
Who with it pass nor know to hope or grieve; —
To man alone 't is given to perceive
That, after all, Fate is no poor misrule,
But rather an inexorable school
Wherein he learns to endure and to achieve.
Yet some there are who learn the first alone,
Supinely learn to bear without complaint:
Better that riskier wisdom gods condone,
Some part to act — as sinner or as saint —
Winning maybe, or, failing, to retreat
Still armed and upright before full defeat.

NEGLECT

"Lofty—still loftier than the world suspects."

THERE was a Book that bore a message kind
From a full heart to an expected friend,
But no such reader chanced this Book to find
And such as read there failed to comprehend:
The title's tarnished now, the leaves are loose,
This clever book has fallen to decay;
Wantonly slighted, warped from long abuse,
None saw the light that on its pages lay.
Yet was its message worthy to be heard
Ere careless touch had blurred what insight penned,
For some faint hint of an inspired word
Clung to the faded pages to the end,—
The aura of some high-born task well done,—
What matters all the rest, neglected One?

IN THE MAKING

"The purpose of life is not happiness but development."

ONE glimpse of beauty ere the clouds o'er-
cast
The rose of dawn! One moment when we
lean
Toward love triumphant till doubts intervene
And in their shadow Love and Dawn go past.
One little glimpse!—and then while life may last
With lowered eyes we plod a toilsome mean,
That which we would and must stand faint between,
Or see our strength by others' strength surpassed.
Yet is there solace for his hampered lot
Whose hurts are laid 'neath patient Nature's spell;
Feast of the eye, thrill of the heart are not
Her purpose set. Sufficient 'tis and well
When pain and joy have borne their fruitage ripe,
She finds within her world some nobler type.

JUDGED BY THE SPHINX

THE Theban Sphinx who watched the road
   along,
   With brooding eyes upon the moving
   mass,
Cried, "Halt! and Guess my Riddle ere you pass—
Why is Truth's quest the Right—all else the
  Wrong?"
In state advanced the leader of the throng—
An autocrat whom none in pomp surpass—
Flatterers and slaves he hears, but not, alas!
The still, small voice which makes the spirit strong.
He cannot answer what the Sphinx demands,
No time has he to judge 'twixt false and true!
"The world needs only him who understands
This difference," quoth the questioner. She grew
Colossal, cried: "Thus, sightless soul, atone!"
And crushed a despot 'gainst her breast of stone.

GEORGE MEREDITH

WITH sovran strength he plied his lofty art,
Touched the world's pulse and felt its tell-
tale beat,
Yet nowise judged Success, nor yet Defeat.
Anon to us he spake; anon, apart;
And balanced held the speculative dart
His genius winged through ancient Forms effete,
Through Pedant, Egoist, and Splendid Cheat,
To sink and quiver in the Modern Heart.
He's gone! But what he wrought's forever Real!
Think of his Child of light condemned to pay
The costs of Love; of Adriatic's breeze
And Otley's sullen waves wherein we feel
The Tragedy of type that lives for aye
In Mad Commander and his French Marquise!

OUT OF THE EAST ,

On the defeat of Italian troops in Abyssinia by Menelek, March 23, 1896.

OUT of the East — like Baal of the past
A thing of fear — a creature of the night,
A Power of Darkness threatening Europe's
light,
Has risen — like a huge Iconoclast!
But noble land there is of resource vast,
And noble race elect to stay this blight:
Already art thou girding for the fight,
O English land! Thy whole heroic past
And crucial present bid thee draw the sword
This battle royal for the world to gain,
And all thy Kinsmen pledge thee Time's reward
For standards bravely borne with cost and pain
Where English valor, conquering, strikes the spark
That lightens all the dull barbaric Dark!

33

VIKINGS

FROM stormy shores, red-bearded Norseman bold,—
From stormy shores over an unknown sea
Thou cam'st,—yet left not to futurity
Record of conflict fierce for power or gold;
No lands despoiled, no captives sought to hold.
Soul-stirred with novel joy! elate with free
Dream of illimitable liberty,—
Thou cam'st,—and went,—thy story strange untold.
Yet still while poets sing they'll celebrate
The fair-haired crew who roamed Rhode Island's shore;
Still with their haunting presence consecrate
Wild Vinland and bleak coast: and, evermore,
On reckless bark which to the gale puts forth,
See phantom Vikings steering for the North.

MY BOOKS

I LOVE you well, beloved! Companions
dear,
There was a time when other friends were
few,
Dull days, dark years through which I found in you
The bread to strengthen and the wine to cheer.
Lewes! 'twas through thy subtle insight clear
I first divined the dispensation new:
Then, Laureate, burst thy vision on my view—
Of "statelier Edens" seen from poet's sphere.
Pale Brontë, and thou stronger woman-soul,
Your patient strength has lightened all my load;
Spencer! thy mighty grasp will ere control
My toiling thought along truth's arduous road.
Each page meets eyes of mine with charmèd looks,
My heart is yours, O little band of books!

GREEK ART

EMBODIED Beauty with indwelling Soul
     Survives in what it wrought; but goddess
      fair
     And columned Temple move us to despair
Of emulation: From beyond the goal
At which we pause, Greek Art surveyed the Whole
Of Life; espoused its Scheme; untrammeled dare
Attempt the heavenly Heights, where blows an air,
Native to those the Muses Nine enroll.
Reverent — not craven — toward the Unknown
    Power
It found and feared not; with serenity
Trusting itself to Growth, as any flower
Unfolds out of an inmost symmetry,
The Art of Greece — untouched by primal ban —
"Pursue Perfection!" cries to downcast Man.

PENALTY

"Pleads for itself the fact—
As Nature, unrepentant, leaves her every act."

O GREAT grey Waves that clamor to the
    shore
    And leap against the cliffs with loud assault
    Of gathered thunders from that mystic
      vault
Whose limits ending still stretch on before;
O lion waves with mad heroic roar
Deafening to meaner sounds 'gainst black basalt
Of frowning cliff!—I count it as the fault
Of partial comprehension to deplore
That law which drives unerring to their bounds
Life's mighty forces—love where love belongs,
Failures, successes—in the unending rounds
Where Nemesis rebukes ancestral wrongs
With penalties, wherefrom no power to save
Between the iron cliff and breaking wave!

SPECULATION

"Sans me plaindre ou m'effrayer,
Je vais où va toute chose,
Où va la feuille de rose
Et la feuille de laurier."

AND is death then a victory or defeat,
Transition unremembered, or the end
Of conscious being, point where Self shall
   blend
With Other, Real and Apparent meet
In that which gives, and takes, and is complete?
Or is this true — as oft you tell me, friend —
What's here amiss by death at last we'll mend;
Through finite pain progression infinite?
Dear Soul! thou sail'st amain but never yet
A resting-place has found for stretchèd wing!
Faint sounds thy call of hope, thy cry of threat,
To other soul that goes not voyaging
But learns, attent, the laws of limits set,
And bends to daily stint, as bow to string.

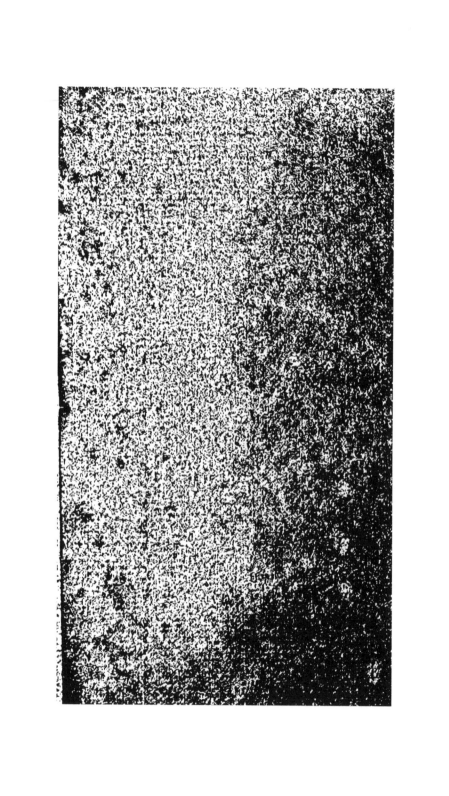